LIVING IN GOD'S FULLNESS

A 30-DAY DEVOTIONAL GUIDE ON
GROWING CLOSER TO GOD AND
HEARING HIS LOVING VOICE

MADELAINA ELIZABETH

"that you may be
filled with all the
fullness of God."

Ephesians 3:19

*Dedicated to my parents
and Jemimah. Who believed in me
when I didn't and who walked
with me on a difficult road,
all while pointing me back to
my first love, Jesus.*

*To anyone else who may be on a
challenging journey, may
this book bring you closer to
the One who is always with you.*

Dear Reader,

My prayer is that you take away a deeper revelation of how to **live in God's fullness**. I have discovered that living in God's fullness means finding all aspects of ourselves **in Him**. Acts 17:28 puts it this way: "for in Him we live and move and have our being."

This book is structured in the way I have experienced God in my quiet time. As I still my heart and mind, I hear Him speak to me in a still small voice to my heart, like the Lord spoke to Elijah in 1 Kings 19:12. Each time I spend this quiet time with God, specific scriptures come to mind that I look up and then I'm able to see an overall message that He is speaking to me. I close in prayer, asking for God's help to give me the ability to do what I cannot on my own.

These 30 days of devotionals are what God has spoken to directly to me in my own quiet time with Him. Knowing that the testimony of Jesus is the spirit of prophecy (Revelations 19:10), I am fully confident that His words to me will also speak to you.

My prayer is that this devotional guide blesses you in your daily life and helps you draw nearer to God and closer to hearing His voice.

Madelaina Elizabeth

Table of Contents:

DAY 1: REMAIN IN HIM

I am the vine and you are the branches. Remain in Me and I will remain in you. From our connectedness, your life will sprout much fruit. But you must remain in Me. Your attentions are caught elsewhere when all I've asked of you is to stay interlocked with Me. I am your foundation, your source of life and nourishment. Through Me flows life and connection to My Spirit. So stay connected to Me and lock your eyes on Me. I ask less of you than you realize.

OI Look up John 15:5 and write it here:

_____

_____

_____

_____

_____

02 Sometimes we try to do things on our own without realizing we are operating apart from Jesus. Is there something in your life that you are trying to accomplish disconnected from Him?

_____

_____

_____

_____

_____

03 Write a prayer to God where you surrender that thing you are trying to accomplish on your own. Instead turn to abiding in Him. Declare that you will be fruitful in that area as you are more connected to Him.

_____

_____

_____

_____

_____

DAY 2: FAITH IN HIM

Step out of that box of safety you have built and take this leap of faith with Me. I promise I will catch you because I've never dropped you before. It's time to step out into the Halls of Faith. There, you can take your place with others who have found My power in their lives through their faith. Why would you doubt when all things are possible with Me?

OI Look up Mark 11:22-23 and write it here:

_____

_____

_____

_____

_____

_____

Jesus tells us to have faith and if we do, even mountains will move. In Matthew 19:26 Jesus says that with God, nothing is impossible.

O2 What areas in your life feel like they are mountains that you believe are impossible to change?

_____

_____

_____

_____

O3 Write down a declaration where you attach your faith to those areas: it is possible with God!

_____

_____

_____

_____

_____

DAY 3: ALIVE IN HIM

There is fullness of life in Me. That means life with joy, happiness, excitement, good things, laughter and fun. Come and walk with Me and I will show you that the drab colors you think life is about are actually a rainbow of colors, meant to be lived with vividness and vibrancy. Experience how I light up your life, filling it with good things - for you are alive in Me!

OI Look up John 10:10 and write it here:

_____

_____

_____

_____

_____

02 In what areas of your life do you see the abundance of Jesus? Why do believe He is there?

_____

_____

_____

03 Pray and thank God for the life and vibrancy you are experiencing because of Him. Invite the Holy Spirit to bring resurrection power into any area you believe God has invited to become more vibrant.

_____

_____

_____

_____

_____

DAY 4: HOPE IN HIM

All My promises are yes and amen. I see the desires of your heart. I am a good God who will bring those desires to fruition. Just look around and see in your life the promises I have already fulfilled. Now look ahead and have hope for what is still is come. For I bring dreams into fulfillment and words into completion.

01   Look up 2 Corinthians 1:20 and write it
     here:

_____

_____

_____

_____

_____

02   What is one promise of God that you
     have seen fulfilled in your life?

_____

_____

_____

_____

03   What is a promise you still believe will
     be fulfilled? Write it down here with a
     prayer of declaration that this promise is
     yes and amen through Christ.

_____

_____

_____

_____

_____

_____

_____

_____

DAY 5: ABUNDANCE IN HIM

I only get better. There is no limit to My goodness. I hear your prayers dear one. I give better and better. More and more. I don't take back, I give more. My hand is generous and always giving. I even try to one-up Myself in My generosity - that is how good I am. So never expect anything less than My very best for My beloved child.

01　Look up Matthew 7:11 and write it here:

_____

_____

_____

_____

_____

02　Do you believe God to be a good Father to you? If no, why not? Oftentimes, our earthly experience defines how we see our heavenly Father.

_____

_____

_____

_____

03　Write a prayer that invites God to reveal Himself to you as a good Father in ways you have never seen before. Ask Him for a good gift for you to experience the reality of Matthew 7:11!

_____

_____

_____

_____

_____

_____

DAY 6: DRINK FROM HIM

Connect to the stream My dear one. I do not give out water the way man thinks. There is an eternal rushing river all around you, and it is filled with all the things that will bring you life. I want you to come to it and drink. Only from that place can you bring My refreshing water to others.

OI   Look up John 4:14 and write it here:

_____

_____

_____

_____

By receiving the water of life from Jesus personally, you learn how to access it and in turn, give it out to others.

02   Was there a time when you experienced the life of Jesus filling you up? And from that place, did you give it out to others?

_____

_____

_____

_____

03   Write a prayer where you ask Jesus to be more aware of the Spirit (water) accessible to you. Then pray for Him to lead you to receive it first, then give it out.

_____

_____

_____

_____

_____

DAY 7: WAIT ON HIM

You always want to rush out ahead of Me and make something happen quickly. But it's always better to go at My pace and wait on My timing. I am working on a plan so much bigger than you can see. Develop the fruit of patience in this waiting season and see it bring you far into My Kingdom. You will not only receive My promises in your life, you will see My Kingdom advance in ways you can't even imagine.

OI   Look up 2 Peter 3:8-9 and write it here:

_____

_____

_____

_____

_____

_____

O2   God has a bigger plan, and this scripture proves it. What is one thing you are waiting on from God?

_____

_____

_____

_____

O3   Write a prayer of surrender to God about that thing you are waiting on. Pray for more grace to develop the fruit of patience. Ask Him to show you vision for the bigger picture regarding the thing you are waiting on.

_____

_____

_____

_____

_____

_____

DAY 8: IDENTITY IN HIM

The solution to your struggles is to discover who you are. You are strong, unshakable, brave, bold, and confident. These things are not because of anything you do but because of who you are in Me. Remember, I am the one who created you and formed you in My image. So remember who you are, the real you.

OI   Look up Isaiah 43:1 and write it here:

_____

_____

_____

_____

This scripture was written for the people of Israel. As believers under the new covenant, this word is ours too.

O2   This scripture says that it is God who formed and shaped you, not your environment, your upbringing or anything else. What parts of yourself come to mind as you contemplate what God has created in you?

_____

_____

_____

_____

O3   Write a prayer thanking God for the ways He created you (be specific!) and ask Him to open your eyes to see more and more how He made you.

_____

_____

_____

_____

DAY 9: SURRENDER TO HIM

I am a big God and I know what I'm doing. I'm bigger than you know. I hold all things together, and it's all in My hands. Do not carry what you are not supposed to carry. You need to surrender it all to Me. I have come to make all that is heavy light, and I want you to trust Me by casting your cares to Me.

OI   Look up 1 Peter 5:7 and write it here:

_____

_____

_____

_____

_____

02   Giving your worries to God can
     sometimes happen second by second!
     What current cares and anxieties come
     to mind?

_____

_____

_____

_____

03   Write a prayer surrendering those
     worries to God, fully releasing them to
     Him. Then practice casting that worry to
     Him whenever it comes up today.

_____

_____

_____

_____

_____

_____

_____

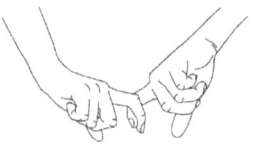

DAY 10: SAFE IN HIM

This is our come away moment, where everything else falls away and our relationship becomes your primary focus. It's all about you and Me, dear one. Feel My delight and My safety. My rest, My safe place. Come back to that place of peace. Nothing you face today will be faced alone. Do not fear, for I am with you. My goodness surely will conquer whatever comes against you. Delight that you are Mine and that I honor you publicly, for I am always near and always by your side.

OI Look up Psalm 23 and write it here:

_____

_____

_____

_____

_____

_____

_____

_____

_____

_____

_____

_____

_____

_____

_____

_____

_____

_____

_____

_____

_____

This scripture is one of the most well-known chapters in the Bible and every verse carries much truth about the nature of God. Pick one verse that is really speaking to you and set it in your mind today. Work at memorizing it so you can reference it in times of need.

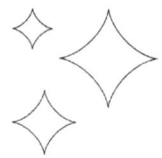

DAY 11: DREAM IN HIM

From Me comes your capacity to dream. I bring life, and I bring vision to you, opening up your eyes to limitless possibility. Where hope had long lay dead and dormant, with My breath I come and awaken in you hope for your future. For the life that lies before you, I have made good plans, plans filled with a future and a hope.

01 Look up Jeremiah 29:11 and write it here:

_____

_____

_____

_____

_____

_____

02 As you read this scripture, what are some "God dreams" in your heart that come to mind?

_____

_____

_____

_____

_____

03 Write a prayer of fresh hope, declaring that God has good plans for your future, including plans to see your dreams come to pass and be fulfilled!

_____

_____

_____

_____

_____

_____

_____

_____

DAY 12: TRUST IN HIM

Never doubt in Me, dear one. Circumstances may make things look impossible but I am on your side. So don't look at the impossibility, look at who I am. And I am a God who never fails you, who bends down from Heaven to move on your behalf. You don't need to do anything more to deserve what I want to do for you. I want to bring miracles into your life, all by My hand, never yours. So trust in Me, trust in who I AM.

OI   Look up Proverbs 3:5 and write it here:

_____

_____

_____

_____

02   Oftentimes we try to strive to attain things in our lives but usually it is because we lack trust that God can do it by His own ability. Is there currently something that comes to mind that you are striving for, not trusting in God's ability?

_____

_____

_____

_____

03   Write a prayer of surrender and ask God to help you trust Him more in that area. Now declare that His ability and goodness will bring to pass what you are believing for!

_____

_____

_____

_____

DAY 13: HEALED IN HIM

Healing is what I paid for on the cross. My sacrifice is what makes it available to you. To access healing is for My kingdom to advance, forcefully. In the midst of pain and darkness, My healing light breaks through. It is My will to heal you. In fact, what I already accomplished on the cross is enough to heal you. So will you come to Me, believing that with Me, your healing is possible?

OI   Look up Isaiah 53:5 and write it here:

_____

_____

_____

This scripture is one of the most well-known healing scriptures, prophesying Jesus' death and the price He paid for our healing.

02   Healing is often needed on many levels - emotionally, mentally, and physically. This scripture shares the truth that Jesus died so that we can be fully healed and restored in all areas. In what areas do you need healing for yourself?

_____

_____

_____

03   Write a prayer inviting Jesus to come heal you. Then write a declaration that by His wounds you are healed. Keep that as a reminder this week.

_____

_____

_____

_____

DAY 14: STRONG IN HIM

You can't be strong all the time. In reality, compared to Me, humans are weak and fragile - facing impossible situations. So let Me be your strength. Let Me be the one to work out what needs to be worked out. The power of My Holy Spirit can do what you cannot. In your weakness, My power is made perfect.

OI   Look up 2 Corinthians 12:9 and write it here:

_____

_____

_____

_____

God's power works best in our weaknesses because He gets the glory in doing what we cannot do alone.

02   Is there something either in you or in your life where you feel very weak?

_____

_____

_____

03   Write a prayer inviting God into that weakness and ask Him to show up and demonstrate His power through you.

_____

_____

_____

_____

_____

_____

DAY 15: VICTORIOUS IN HIM

You must remember to always factor Me into the equation, because it changes the results. You're not on your own, you're with Me - the most powerful being and force on the planet. I am a good God and have good things in store for you. As I do My work in you, you must continue to trust Me and trust My leading. For it is My mighty hand that is in your life.

OI Look up Romans 8:31 and write it here:

_____
_____
_____
_____
_____

O2 Have you had a situation happen in your life where you knew God was with you and saw Him intervene on your behalf? If so, when?

_____
_____
_____
_____
_____

O3 Write a prayer that invites God to continue to open your eyes to His involvement and nearness in your life.

_____
_____
_____
_____
_____
_____

DAY 16: CO-LABOR WITH HIM

Walk with Me and learn from Me, experience My unforced rhythms of grace. There is no more demand on you, it is only the enemy trying to get you to overwork and over-strive for everything. But My yoke is easy and what I require of you is light. I am teaching you My ways, where there is fruit in your labors and rest for your soul.

OI Look up Matthew 11:29-30 and write it here:

_____
_____
_____
_____

O2 When we live life in God's way, what we do should not feel like a burden. Instead, it should be a joy! Are there areas of your life where you know you are co-laboring with God? Any areas where you feel you are trying to work independent of Him?

_____
_____
_____
_____

O3 Write a prayer inviting God to come and teach you how to work with Him, how to be yoked to Him. Exchange whatever feels heavy from strife with His freedom and lightness.

_____
_____
_____
_____

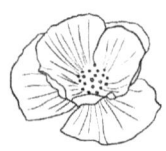

DAY 17: FORGIVENESS IN HIM

Forgiveness is not something you do for the sake of others, it is something you do as a response for what I did for you. You cannot live your life harboring grudges against others who have wronged you. It will only keep you in bondage. Receive the debt that I have paid for you, then know how to extend it toward others. Let Me deal with the justice of your cause because remember, vengeance is Mine.

OI Look up Matthew 18:33 and write it here:

_____

_____

_____

This scripture is from the Parable of the Unforgiving Servant, where Jesus talks about a servant who could not forgive a man who owed him money even after the servant was forgiven a greater debt.

02 We can only forgive others when we have a revelation of how much God has forgiven us. Write a list of what you have been forgiven.

_____

_____

_____

03 Whether or not we feel it, we can choose to forgive by releasing something in our heart and expressing forgiveness. Leave the justice of your situation to God! Write a prayer of forgiveness for anyone who comes to mind.

_____

_____

_____

_____

DAY 18: GOOD FROM HIM

You don't always see My divine protection even in the midst of storms. So when trials arrive, I urge you to not say "Why God?" but "Yes God, I trust what you'll do with this." This makes a fool of the enemy. Because all he ever does is try to separate you from Me, questioning Me. But let's prove him wrong by drawing closer to Me in this season - trusting Me in every little thing, even the things that seemingly go wrong.

OI   Look up Romans 8:28 and write it here:

_____

_____

_____

_____

02   God causes EVERYTHING to work
together for good. Have you seen a
situation work together for good? Is
there one you're still waiting on?

_____

_____

_____

_____

03   If you have a situation in which you are
still waiting to see things work together
for good, write it here, declaring that
God will work it for good. Have eyes to
see God move on your behalf.

_____

_____

_____

_____

_____

DAY 19: PRESENT WITH HIM

Don't worry so much about what is ahead. Just focus on the now and today and trust that I am in your tomorrow. I am in your details where I am actively working things together for good. You don't have to work for anything. Just abide, just be with Me. It's what I do, not what you do. Now is the time to stay present, holding the future with hope.

OI Look up Matthew 6:34 and write it here:

_____

_____

_____

_____

_____

O2 Do you find your mind wandering into tomorrow, thinking about things in the future? What are some of those things coming to mind right now? List them below.

_____

_____

_____

_____

O3 Write a prayer, surrendering to God any worries about tomorrow. Then thank Him for today and ask Him to help you stay present in today.

_____

_____

_____

_____

_____

_____

DAY 20: CARRIED BY HIM

You are looking for validation of your pain from others, trying to find purpose in it from what other people will say or do. But I am the one who understands. I know all, I see all and I endured the greatest suffering of all. I carried your pain and I want to carry it even now. I am the only one who will truly know your pain. So will you give it to Me? Because I am the one able to make beauty from ashes and joy from mourning.

01 Look up 2 Corinthians 4:17 and write it
    here:

    _____

    _____

    _____

    _____

    _____

02 Have you had pain in your life? Painful
    moments? List them below:

    _____

    _____

    _____

    _____

    Jesus knows what you're going through
    and what you've been through! He
    wants to carry that pain for you.

03 Write a prayer inviting Jesus into that
    pain and write a declaration that Jesus
    will make beauty from your ashes.
    (Isaiah 61:3)

    _____

    _____

    _____

    _____

    _____

DAY 21: PEACE IN HIM

Your source of peace comes not from the outside world, for the outside world is only able to dictate the ebb and flow of peace based on circumstances. But My peace that I give you is not from this world. My heavenly peace supersedes any worldly circumstance and gives you peace of mind and heart, despite what is going on. My peace is the ruling force over this earth, and when you partner with Me, your Prince of Peace, that force will rule over you, despite what is going on around you in this earthly world.

OI   Look up John 14:27 and write it here:

_____

_____

_____

_____

_____

02   Has there been a time when Jesus revealed to you that He was Prince of Peace (Isaiah 9:6), giving you overwhelming peace, in the middle of a tumultuous external circumstance?

_____

_____

_____

_____

_____

03   Write a prayer inviting Jesus to reveal Himself even more as Prince of Peace in your life. Take a moment to clear your mind and breathe, choosing to encounter His peace in this moment.

_____

_____

_____

_____

_____

_____

DAY 22: MERCY FROM HIM

Don't look back at the mistakes in life that you regret. It does you no good to beat yourself up about them. People always forget that I am generous in mercy, pouring out pools available to anyone who wants to come and drink. Come to Me with any guilt and let Me wash you clean with My waters of forgiveness, for I am a merciful God who never keeps a record of your wrongs up in Heaven.

OI Look up Exodus 34:6-7a and write it here:

_____

_____

_____

_____

_____

Guilt very often leads us away from
Jesus, but it should lead us to the cross
where He paid for our freedom from
condemnation.

O2 There is mercy and forgiveness for you!
Are there things in your past or in your
present that you believe you need
mercy for? Write them below.

_____

_____

_____

_____

O3 Write a prayer asking God to help you
receive His mercy for what is causing
you guilt. Declare that He is slow to
anger and forgives all sin.

_____

_____

_____

_____

DAY 23: WALK WITH HIM

It may feel that the road you are walking on is dim and dark. You may even feel that you have lost your way. But rest assured, I am right there with you, holding your hand. Sometimes you may not see the full picture of what I am up to, and that's okay. Now is the time to more deeply trust Me and have faith in Me, because I know the way, even if you can't see it. So reach out and hold My hand. We'll walk this road together.

OI Look up Psalm 119:105 and write it here:

_____

_____

_____

_____

John 1:1 tells us that Jesus is the Word.
Looking at 119:105, it God's written word
and the living Word that guides us.

02 Have you ever had a time where you felt
lost in life? How did you encounter God
guiding you, if any?

_____

_____

_____

03 If there are any places in your life that
you feel lost now, write a prayer inviting
God to be the light to your path and for
Jesus to reveal Himself to guide you.

_____

_____

_____

_____

_____

DAY 24: FRIEND IN HIM

You are not alone, for I am always by your side. Your faithful companion, your ever-present aide. I am the best friend you will ever know, for I am constant, consistent, loving, patient and kind. As you receive all these things from Me, you will start to see others begin to surround you as near and dear friends because you will be able to give out the love and generosity that you receive from Me.

01 Look up John 15:15 and write it here:

_____

_____

_____

_____

_____

02 What does it mean to you for Jesus to call you friend? Have you experienced Him as a friend before?

_____

_____

_____

_____

03 Sometimes our own hurts in friendships keep us from seeing Jesus as the true friend that He is. Write a prayer surrendering any past pain and invite Jesus to reveal Himself to you as a friend.

_____

_____

_____

_____

_____

_____

DAY 25: SIT WITH HIM

You give and you give, thinking you please Me by what you do for others. But I tell you, you please Me by what you do unto Me. Yes, I delight in your good works for others but I am most focused on your heart and where you stand with Me. All your doing won't get you as far as simply being with me and surrendering all that you have into My hands. Choosing to sit with Me is like a fragrant aroma, precious in My eyes, and it will never be taken from you.

OI Look up Luke 10:41-42 and write it here:

_____

_____

_____

_____

_____

The story of Mary and Martha is well known. As Martha does all that she thinks needs to be done, Mary sits at His feet. Jesus commends Mary and tells Martha that her worries aren't what really matters.

O2 We all, at some point, prioritize "doing" over sitting at Jesus' feet. Do you remember a time when you have done this? Was there a time when you prioritized sitting with Jesus instead?

_____

_____

_____

_____

O3 Write a prayer of surrender, giving God all the times you "did" versus "sat." Ask Him to help you choose the important thing more and more.

_____

_____

_____

DAY 26: PROTECTED IN HIM

I tell you once again, do not fear, for I am with you. There is a reason I say it so often to My people, for many have not experienced the true reality of My nearness. It means no harm will come your way. It means that where you go, My divine protection follows you. I am sorry for the times you did not feel like you experienced that reality, but I encourage you to lean into Me once again, believing that My reality of protection exists for you. You are My child and I will do whatever it takes to keep you safe.

OI   Look up Psalm 91:2 and write it here:

_____

_____

_____

_____

Oftentimes our current life experiences create blocks for our belief of truth of God's word.

O2   When you read the above verse or even the entire Psalm 91, are you able to receive these truths or do objections rise up within you?

_____

_____

_____

O3   Write a prayer surrendering your past experiences that have caused you to not believe God's promise of protection and then invite Him to show you that reality.

_____

_____

_____

_____

_____

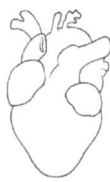

DAY 27: LIFE IN HIM

Let Me shine through those storm clouds in your life and lift the heaviness that plagues you. Depression and hopelessness is not of Me. In fact, I am the opposite - I am life! So let Me pour out the life waters of My spirit into you. Where you feel dry and barren, I will spring to life! Like waters in a desert. Only I have the power to spring up new life out of a dead land. So do not lose hope, for I will certainly bring all parts of you back to life!

OI Look up Isaiah 43:20 and write it here:

_____

_____

_____

_____

God making rivers in a wasteland is also a promise of God bringing life to the dead parts of our being.

02 Do you feel dark clouds over you? Or perhaps in a specific area of your life? What are the lies that are speaking against hope in you?

_____

_____

_____

_____

03 Write a prayer inviting God to pour out His life waters into those dark and hopeless areas. Write a declaration that you will experience light and hope within you!

_____

_____

_____

_____

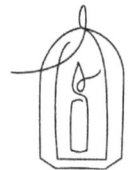

DAY 28: EMPOWERED BY HIM

Let Me move in your life in a powerful way. You may doubt the decision you are making in this very moment but I tell you, you are making the right choice and taking the right step. You don't always need to know what's on the other side of your decisions to know if its the right one. In fact, you don't always need incredibly clear direction from Me when you make decisions. Don't worry, I will guide you if you go too far off the path. Trust yourself and trust how I made you.

OI Look up Proverbs 16:9 and write it here:

_____

_____

_____

_____

This scripture talks about the dynamic of us making plans and God still having the oversight of our way. We do not have to be frozen all the time waiting for a sign from God to move.

O2 Are you having a hard time making a decision right now? What is making it difficult?

_____

_____

_____

O3 Write a prayer surrendering any worry about making the wrong decision and ask for God to guide you and also to give you the confidence to make a decision, trusting that He has oversight over it all.

_____

_____

_____

_____

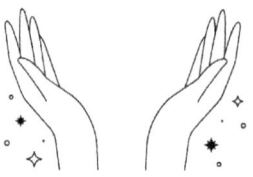

DAY 29: THANKFUL FOR HIM

You already live in My goodness, you just need to open your eyes and see it. Every little thing you have desired, I have made true or am making come true. You cannot let big pieces of negativity block you from seeing the blessings in your life. Your attitude, your thoughts and your words are under your power to control. You have the power to walk free from the negative. Choose to thank Me for all the good. Gratitude is the key to shifting your focus back onto Me.

OI Look up Psalm 106:1 and write it here:

_____

_____

_____

_____

Sometimes our words can be self-fulfilling prophecies, and it is up to us to make the choice to switch from the negative to the positive, choosing to look at and be thankful for the good.

O2 Is there something in your life that you are struggling to see God's goodness in?

_____

_____

_____

_____

_____

O3 Instead of focusing on the current negative, choose to shift your eyes to seeing the good. Write a list of the good things in your life that you are thankful for. Challenge yourself to add 10 more this week to your list!

_____

_____

_____

_____

DAY 30: FEAST IN HIM

No more settling, no more thinking that what you have is good enough. No! That is not what you're worth and it's not who I am. I prepare a feast in the presence of your enemies, not just a one-course meal. An abundance, an extravagance - I am not a God of the okay or just good enough. I am a perfect, all-knowing God who has surprises and twists and turns for you, all of them for the better. So increase your expectations for all that I have for you.

OI Look up Psalm 23:5 and write it here:

02 Are there promises from God you are still believing for? Have you begun to settle for less thank you should in your expectations for them to come to pass?

03 Write a prayer where you reinvigorate your hopes and expectations for God to bring you a feast in all areas of your life, especially for the promises you are still believing for.

FINAL THOUGHTS

My charge to you after having completed these 30 days is to keep the momentum! Continue to take time each day to hear God's voice, whether it is a still small voice in your heart, a thought that comes to your mind, or even an image. Pay attention because God speaks to everyone differently. I encourage you to revisit the devotionals that really spoke to you, to go back through the scriptures and even choose a few memory verses that can help you stay connected to God and living in His fullness.

I would also encourage you to download the free YouVersion Bible app if you haven't already. That way, you can compare different Bible translations. I like to read my Bible in NLT and I also look at NKJV, AMP, TPT and MSG to see different ways the scripture is translated.

Most importantly, continue to remember that living in God's fullness comes from what you find in Him. He is your source and your everything. Continue to meditate on that truth and you will find that the fullness and prosperity of His love abounds in you!

Madelaina Elizabeth

ABOUT ME

Having always had a dream of writing, it is my pleasure and my joy to be able to publish this devotional guide as my first book. I have been walking with Jesus since I was little, but it wasn't until January 2019 that I gave Him my whole life.

This devotional guide is fruit of my "yes" to God and all that we've walked through together. He has been so good and so faithful to me, awakening dreams in my heart and breathing hope into places I once thought, were dead.

I now live in sunny Redding, CA, with my sister-best friend and my two cats. I enjoy hiking, kayaking, paddleboarding, golfing, running, gardening, writing and cooking. I have the privilege of being a member at my dream church, Bethel and am excited for all the opportunities yet to come with my creativity and writing!

Let's be *friends!*

 @madelainaelizabeth

www.madelainaelizabeth.com

*"Writing all purposed to help
lift your eyes."*

...

Explore more daily reminders at our store:

BARNABÉ STUDIO

Barnabé Studio is a collective of creatives charged with the vision to release God's creativity into the world. Barnabé Studio sells a variety of handmade gifts and home decor on Etsy.